WHAT HAPPENED HERE?

ANGLO SAXON VILLAGE

Books are to be returned on or before the l...

Monica Stoppleman

Photographs by Maggie Murray
Illustrations by Gillian Clements

Contents

A & C BLACK · LONDON

46851

Anglo-Saxon village

This book is about Stow, a village built over 1500 years ago by Anglo-Saxon settlers. The village is in the part of England known as East Anglia, which means the 'eastern part of the Angles' land'. The children in this book wanted to find out what life was like in the village in Anglo-Saxon times. They went to visit the site which is now known as West Stow Anglo-Saxon Village.

In the Visitor Centre the children discovered that Stow is the only Anglo-Saxon village in the world which has been reconstructed on its original site. Outside in the village they found people building houses using the same tools and materials as we think the Anglo-Saxons did. You can read about the history of Stow in the time-line on pages 6 and 7.

The children started their investigation by doing a tour of the village. They studied their site guide and listened to a taped commentary which seemed to bring the village back to life.

pigs rooting for acorns

woodland (which provided timber for building)

(trade path used since Stone Age Times)

hurdle

sedge and reeds (used for thatching)

willow (used for weaving into baskets and hurdles)

Icknield Way

net

Acc. 468.51
Class 942.012 STO T.S.C.
S

2

The picture shows the village of Stow and the land around as it might have looked in about AD 500.

short grass (good for grazing sheep)

clay pit

spelt wheat for bread

fallow land

barley

weaving house

oven

hall

workshop

living house

clay left here in the air and rain to become more workable

pole lathe

hen house

wood working area

clay weathering area

wet land (good for grazing cattle)

River Lark

How do we know about the Anglo-Saxon village?

There are no written records from early Anglo-Saxon times. The archaeologists who excavated Stow used evidence they discovered to piece together a picture of life in the village. Sometimes they found it helpful to compare the evidence at Stow with discoveries made at other Anglo-Saxon sites.

The archaeologists who excavated Stow found this Anglo-Saxon skeleton in a cemetery nearby. During this period most Anglo-Saxons were buried with their treasured possessions. Archaeologists think that those with nothing in their graves were probably slaves.

Objects
Many whole objects and over a million fragments of animal bones were found at Stow. Marks on some of these finds helped the archaeologists work out what tools, materials and techniques the villagers had used.

Underground evidence

Evidence in the soil around a find is just as important as the find itself. Marks found in the soil at Stow showed where posts which had held up the buildings had rotted away. Marks in the soil also showed the positions of pits under the buildings. From this and other evidence, the archaeologists were able to work out the size, shape and number of buildings in the village.

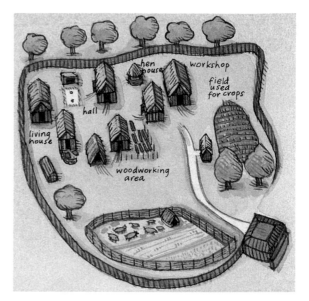

This is a plan of the reconstructed Anglo-Saxon village at West Stow.

Reconstruction

The archaeologists pieced together many thousands of clues to show how the Anglo-Saxons of Stow may have gone about their daily lives. They decided to reconstruct some buildings to test their ideas.

▲
Stow is an experimental village where the staff try out the archaeologists' ideas. They are still finding out what works and what doesn't. At first the archaeologists thought that Anglo-Saxons might have built the walls of their houses out of split logs and filled the gaps with mud. But when this was tried, it didn't work very well. The mud dried, shrank and fell out.

Another house was built with walls made of ▶ interlocking planks. The planks are made from tree trunks split lengthways. Each plank is wedge-shaped and slots snugly into the next. The children discovered that this type of wall is draught-proof. They thought that houses built in this way would be strong and warm.

Time-lines

The first time-line shows some of the important events which took place during Anglo-Saxon times. The second time-line shows some of the important events in the history of West Stow, up to the present day.

Main events, ideas and inventions

AD 340

AD 340–370 Roman Britain under attack from Picts and Scots in the north, and Saxons in the east.

The Romans pay some Saxons to fight in the Roman army. Some of these Saxons settle in Britain.

AD 410 Small groups of Angles, Saxons, Jutes, Franks and Frisians cross the North Sea.

AD 410–450 Small, scattered Anglo-Saxon villages built in eastern, central and southern England.

Roman law and order breaks down.

The Anglo-Saxons speak their own language which is now called Old English. The Anglo-Saxons worship their own gods. Anglo-Saxons did not write their ideas down but shared them by word of mouth.

Many Roman ideas are ignored or rejected.

Anglo-Saxon groups take over the old Roman fields and farm them.

AD 550 Anglo-Saxons begin to spread into western Britain.

Large numbers of Anglo-Saxon tribal leaders means there are lots of royal families. The tribes all have similar customs and practices.

AD 597 Augustine, a missionary sent by Pope Gregory in Rome to convert the Anglo-Saxons to Christianity, lands in Kent.

Some Anglo-Saxon kings become Christian. Anglo-Saxons continue to worship both pagan and Christian gods for several generations.

Events at Stow

AD 420

AD 420 The first Anglo-Saxon settlers arrive at Stow. First houses and halls built.

Skilled blacksmiths, potters and boneworkers come to the village regularly.

Soon after **AD 600** the villagers begin to drift away from Stow.

About **AD 650** the village of Stow is finally abandoned.

The abandoned village of Stow falls into decay and is forgotten. The people who live nearby continue to farm the old Anglo-Saxon fields.

1300 The fields around Stow vanish under a thick layer of sand blown over them by a great sand storm.

1849–1852 Anglo-Saxon cemetery with skeletons and burial urns found 400 yards from Stow.

Some Anglo-Saxons learn Christian reading and writing, which is in Latin.

Anglo-Saxons build Christian churches in East Anglia.

By **AD 600** several Anglo-Saxon kingdoms established including East Anglia, Northumbria, Mercia, Essex, Middlesex, Kent, Wessex and Sussex.

Early AD 600s The first Anglo-Saxon towns appear including Gippeswic (Ipswich) and Hamwic (Southampton).

Trade with countries abroad increases.

Jewels and precious metals imported from Asia and Mediterranean countries. Beautiful jewelled work produced for kings.

AD 625 Sutton Hoo ship buried. Raedwald, King of East Anglia, dies. He is later mentioned by the historian Bede as a very powerful king, known as King of all England.

The Sutton Hoo king (possibly King Raedwald) is buried with some Christian objects in his grave as well as the other objects which showed he had continued to believe in Anglo-Saxon gods.

AD 616–633 East Anglia is the most powerful Anglo-Saxon kingdom.

AD 672–735 Bede lives and works as a monk in Northumbria.

AD 731 Bede writes his book *The History of the English Church and People*. It is the first history of Britain.

AD 775 Mercia is the most powerful kingdom in England. Offa, king of Mercia, claims to be King of all England.

Offa introduces the silver penny. This is the first use of money as we know it since Roman times.

AD 793 The first Viking raids on England.

1940s Local archaeologist Basil Brown finds Anglo-Saxon pottery fragments kicked up by burrowing rabbits, whilst out walking. He announces the existence of a site.

1965–72 Stanley West and a team of archaeologists begin to excavate Stow.

The layer of sand over the site has preserved pits and post holes in the soil. The team excavates the sites of many Anglo-Saxon houses.

1972 The West Stow Anglo-Saxon Trust is set up to build an experimental village. The aim is to test out ideas about how the Anglo-Saxons built their houses.

1973 The first reconstructed house is built. Later more buildings forming a hall and house group are built.

1979 The site is opened to visitors.

1988 The Visitor Centre is added and opened.

Who lived in the village?

The children interviewed some members of a 'living history' group. The actors were visiting Stow, playing the part of an Anglo-Saxon family. The first interview was with Grandfather Aelfric who is 55. As one of the older villagers, his skills and knowledge are highly valued by the others. Aelfric explained that none of the villagers needed to read or write because they show, or tell each other, everything they need to know.

These actors are members of a 'living history' group which sometimes visits Stow. The actors dress in Anglo-Saxon costumes and call themselves by Anglo-Saxon names. From left to right they are Hengist and Coelnoth, who are brothers, Ealswith and baby, and her children Aelfmaer, Cuthrun, Aelfwynn, Aethelflaed and Grandfather Aelfric.

Ealswith is married to Coelnoth, Aelfric's son. Ealswith came from the nearby village of Lackford to marry Coelnoth at the age of 14. She is very happy at Stow because there is usually plenty to eat.

Ealswith showed the children one of the marriage gifts Coelnoth gave her. It is a beautiful brooch. Ealswith believes that the marks on the back of the brooch are a good luck charm but Coelnoth said he thought they were the maker's name.

Ealswith has five children. She is worried about little Aelfmaer. He is often ill and wants to stay inside the house wrapped in a blanket. Ealswith explained that although she prays to the goddess who looks after the sick, she knows that one or two of her children may not live to be grown up. Ealswith is looking forward to the feast to be held in the evening. She hopes the family will talk and sing of the old days.

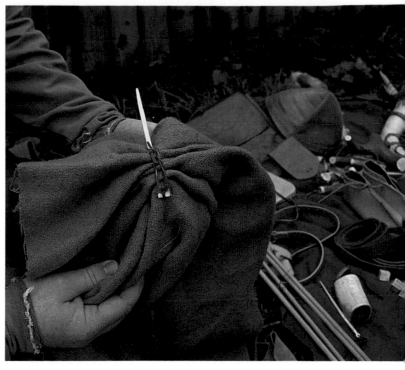

The members of the 'living history' group visit markets held at Stow to sell replica Anglo-Saxon goods they make.

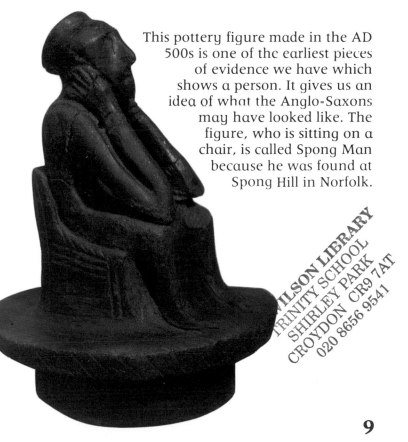

This pottery figure made in the AD 500s is one of the earliest pieces of evidence we have which shows a person. It gives us an idea of what the Anglo-Saxons may have looked like. The figure, who is sitting on a chair, is called Spong Man because he was found at Spong Hill in Norfolk.

WILSON LIBRARY
TRINITY SCHOOL
SHIRLEY PARK
CROYDON CR9 7AT
020 8656 9541

9

Where did the villagers come from?

The children learned that the Angles and the Saxons were two tribes from the countries we now call Germany and Denmark. During the Roman occupation of Britain some Angles and Saxons came here to fight for the Romans. They were rewarded with land on which to settle.

By about AD 410, most of the Roman soldiers had left Britain. More Angles and Saxons rowed across the North Sea in large, shallow-bottomed boats. They were farmers who wanted to settle in Britain. Their own lands were being flooded by the sea and their villages were being attacked by fierce tribes.

Britain during the AD 400s. This map shows where the Angles and Saxons came from, and some of the places in which they settled. In some places there was fighting and many Britons fled westwards. In other places the Angle and Saxon settlers mixed peacefully with the Roman Britons. They all intermingled to become 'Anglo-Saxons'.

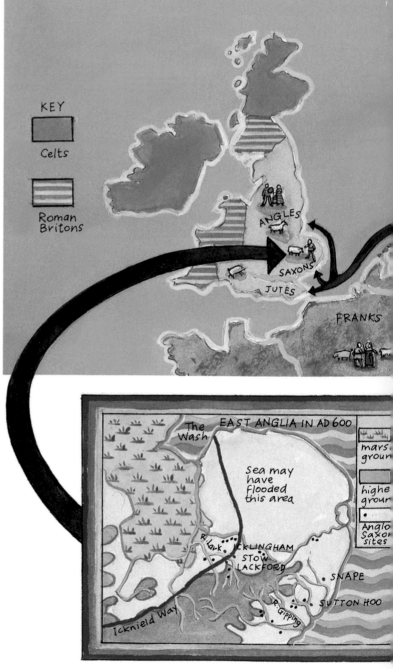

KEY

Celts

Roman Britons

ANGLES

SAXONS

JUTES

FRANKS

EAST ANGLIA IN AD 600

The Wash

Sea may have flooded this area

marsh groun

highe groun

Anglo Saxor sites

R. Lark

ICKLINGHAM
STOW
LACKFORD

SNAPE

R. Gipping

SUTTON HOO

Icknield Way

When they reached the coast of Britain, the Angles and Saxons followed the rivers inland. One group reached the site at Stow. The farmers saw untended Roman fields which they knew they could farm with the tools they had brought. There was plenty of wood for building and for fuel, and good grazing for animals.

The children learned that no traces of boats used by the settlers in East Anglia have been found. They thought that the farmers who came to Stow might not have had their own boats. Perhaps the farmers persuaded people who lived by the sea to ferry them across the North Sea.

The Anglo-Saxon settlers built their village on a low hill to the north of the River Lark. The name Stow simply means 'place'.

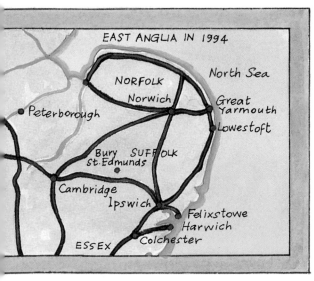

Building the village

Having chosen the site for their village, the Anglo-Saxon settlers started to build. The two main materials they used were wood and plants. They cut down oak, ash, hazel and hornbeam trees with axes. They split the trunks where they fell, making planks and posts which they carried back to the village. They may have had carts and oxen to help with the work. In the village they shaped the newly cut or 'green' wood while it was soft.

In the woodworking area the children watched a site worker use a wooden wedge to split a log in the same way as an Anglo-Saxon carpenter would have done. Anglo-Saxon children learned building skills at an early age by watching the carpenters at work.

The villagers made the most of their valuable timber supply by 'coppicing', or farming, the woods. Trees were cut so they would grow back in a way that would provide a plentiful supply of timber. None of the wood was wasted. The villagers used wood to make nearly everything in their village including houses, furniture and household objects. Dead branches were collected for firewood. Huge amounts of timber were needed to be made into charcoal. Blacksmiths used the charcoal, which burns much hotter than wood, to soften lumps of iron which they hammered into tools and weapons.

The settlers found other useful building materials, such as sedge and reeds for making thatched roofs, lining the river bank. They used the long bendy branches of willow trees to weave into hurdles and baskets.

The Anglo-Saxons split their logs lengthways along the grain. A skilful carpenter could split many planks from one tree trunk. Planks split in this way are much stronger than planks which are sawn.

These children tried weaving hurdles from thin willow branches in very much the same way as the Anglo-Saxons of Stow would have done. The villagers probably used the hurdles, which could be moved around very easily, to control where animals grazed.

Inside a house

Archaeologists know from their excavations that there were three groups of houses in the Anglo-Saxon village of Stow. Each group was made up of 'living houses' and workshops clustered around a hall.

The archaeologists have reconstructed two of the groups. They don't know exactly what any of the buildings at Stow looked like above ground level because the timbers rotted away hundreds of years ago. But they found pieces of charred oak planks, hazel sticks and burnt thatch which were left when one of the buildings burned down in Anglo-Saxon times. These remains gave them useful clues about what the buildings may have looked like.

The children visited one of the reconstructed 'living houses'. They learned that a family of up to 10 people would have lived and slept here. Other relations lived in neighbouring houses, making up a single family group of about 35 people.

The members of each family group met together in their own hall to eat, make music and discuss important matters. They shared the workshops with their close relations. All the villagers farmed the nearby land together.

This boy discovered that a sturdy frame supports the thatched roof of this house. The frame is made of thick, vertical ash poles with thinner hazel rods running from side to side, tied across the ash poles.

There was one big room inside the living house where the whole family slept and lived. This is the kind of bed they may have slept on. The children tried it out and found it was quite comfy. You can see one corner of the small firebox on the left. Some food was cooked on this, but big meals were cooked in the hall. The living house was kept warm by the burning logs in the firebox.

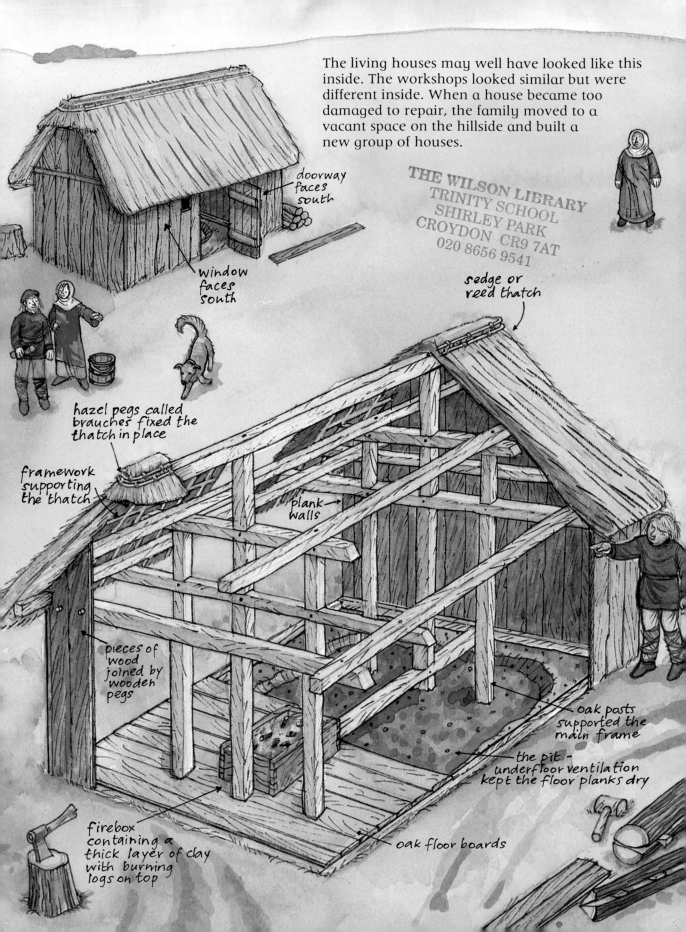

The living houses may well have looked like this inside. The workshops looked similar but were different inside. When a house became too damaged to repair, the family moved to a vacant space on the hillside and built a new group of houses.

doorway faces south

window faces south

THE WILSON LIBRARY
TRINITY SCHOOL
SHIRLEY PARK
CROYDON CR9 7AT
020 8656 9541

sedge or reed thatch

hazel pegs called brauches fixed the thatch in place

framework supporting the thatch

plank walls

pieces of wood joined by wooden pegs

oak posts supported the main frame

the pit – underfloor ventilation kept the floor planks dry

firebox containing a thick layer of clay with burning logs on top

oak floor boards

Heating, lighting and keeping clean

The children noticed that the doors and windows of all the houses in the village faced south. They guessed this was to let in as much light as possible. Fresh air also came in through the windows which had no glass in them. At night the only light inside the house came from candles made from animal fat, or from the fire.

The children found that log fires did make the houses warm inside. But they thought that the burning wood made the air very smoky. We know from Anglo-Saxon skeletons that the villagers were very troubled by coughs and blocked noses. The children wondered if this was caused by breathing in so much smoke from fires.

The river played an important part in life at Stow. People washed themselves and their clothes in the river. They may have used soapwort, a plant which makes a lather, or soap they made from ashes, animal fat and urine.

They took all their drinking and cooking water from the river, carrying it in wooden buckets up to the village. The children tried this for themselves and found it was very hard work.

The villagers went to the toilet in the wood, well away from the river. This saved them from diseases caused by drinking foul water. Even so, they did become ill from time to time.

The villagers treated themselves with herbs which grew wild around Stow. They used tiny amounts of bracken, which is poisonous when eaten in large quantities, to get rid of worms from the gut. All the villagers had fleas and lice, and itching was normal.

Experiments can be a useful way of learning from the past. The children tried washing up without water as the Anglo-Saxons might have done. They found sand and ashes from the fire cleaned wooden bowls well. You could try this out.

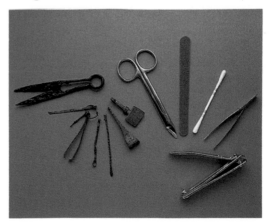

The objects on the left are Anglo-Saxon. They were buried in an Anglo-Saxon grave. The ones on the right are the modern versions. Can you match them up?

Working the land

All the food which the Anglo-Saxons ate had either to be grown by them or picked in the wild. Their year was ruled by the seasons. In spring they dug ditches and sowed seeds, beans, flax and herbs. In summer they spread manure, mended fences and hurdles, made fish traps, sheared sheep, cut firewood and weeded.

The girls planted field beans using replica wooden Anglo-Saxon tools. They found it was back-breaking work. Behind them, spelt wheat is starting to shoot. The Anglo-Saxons grew this for flour.

In autumn the Anglo-Saxons reaped, picked dye plants, beat the flax, roofed, thatched, slaughtered animals to eat in winter, and cut hay for animal feed. In winter they ploughed, threshed, cut wood, split timber, pruned the orchards and did indoor jobs.

These girls tried threshing and separating spelt wheat. They used a long wooden thwacker, or flail to bash the ripe wheat grains off the stalks and split the husks. They threw the mixture of grain and husks into the air using a round, cloth-covered tray called a winnowing fan. The husks blew away in the wind, and the grains landed back in the fan.

Everyone helped with the work. Some of the heaviest jobs were probably done by the slaves. The villagers of Stow grew more than enough food to feed themselves. They traded what was left over for other goods such as iron for their tools, beads and brooches.

This picture of Anglo-Saxon life comes from a calendar called 'The Labour of the Months' which was written and illustrated between AD 1000 and AD 1100. It shows ploughing in Solmonath, the month we know as January.

Using animals

Pigs were the most important animals to the very first villagers. Pigs had big litters which meant the village had plenty of meat. Sheep and goats, which gave milk and wool as well as meat, grazed the land which was not suitable for cattle or pigs.

▲
Feeding pigs in the Anglo-Saxon month of Wintirfyllith, which we call September. The villagers got most of their meat from the animals they raised. They ate a few wild animals and caught fish from the river.

These Tamworth pigs are the closest ▶ modern breed to Anglo-Saxon pigs. They are very strong so this boy stayed well behind the electrified fence while he fed them.

As time went by the villagers raised more cattle, and pigs became less important. Cattle provided milk as well as meat. Their hides, horns, bones and sinews could also be used. The villagers cut horns to use as drinking cups from cows they killed for meat. They made the hides into leather for shoes. The villagers also kept a small number of horses to ride and oxen to pull their carts.

The villagers made many useful small items, such as dice, pins and needles, from cattle bones and from antlers shed by wild deer. Many fine-toothed combs were found at Stow. Some may have been used as nit combs. Making combs involved skilled sawing and riveting, and may have been done by travelling boneworkers who came to the village.

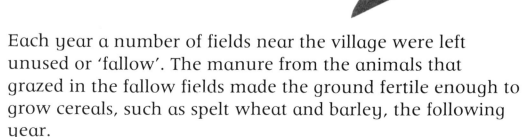

Each year a number of fields near the village were left unused or 'fallow'. The manure from the animals that grazed in the fallow fields made the ground fertile enough to grow cereals, such as spelt wheat and barley, the following year.

Preparing, storing and cooking food

The children investigated how the villagers made bread. They learned that the grain was made into flour with a hand mill called a quern. Each quern had two millstones made of hard rock which ground the grain into flour. After milling, the flour was sieved to remove grit and dirt. The more the flour was sieved, the finer it was and the better bread it made. The most important villagers ate the best bread. Poor people added ground acorns and even weed seeds to make their flour go further.

This girl tried baking bread in a replica clay oven at Stow. The site worker lit a fire inside. When the oven was hot, he raked out the ashes. The girl put the flat bread in, and the site worker sealed the oven. The oven stayed hot enough to cook the bread.

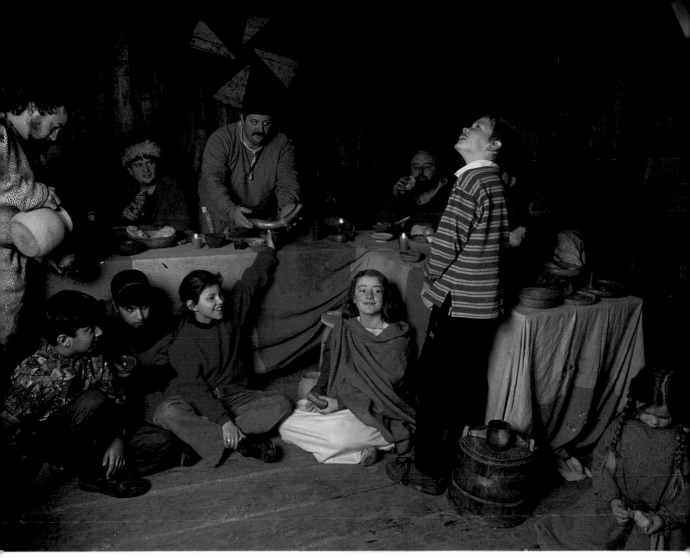

When the villagers wanted to celebrate or give thanks to their gods, they held a feast in the hall. They might have drunk barley beer and eaten roast meats, fruit, and honey-sweetened bread flavoured with spices or seeds. People told riddles, played board games, made music and sang of the brave deeds of their ancestors.

Nowadays we have fridges, freezers and cans in which to store food. Food which is out of season here is brought from abroad and sold in our markets and shops. The Anglo-Saxons had different methods for preserving food over the winter months. They dried vegetables, fungi and herbs. They smoked or salted meat and fish. They pickled foods in various liquids, including honey. The villagers had to work hard to keep mice, rats, insects and mould out. Pests could ruin an entire harvest.

Spinning and weaving

The villagers of Stow made all their own cloth. They used it to make clothes and blankets. They even made tablecloths. Ordinary people wore clothes made of wool or linen. The archaeologists know a lot about how the villagers made cloth because they found traces of cloth and many different tools for making cloth at Stow. They used this evidence to reconstruct an Anglo-Saxon weaving house.

In the weaving house the children used wooden drop spindles just as the Anglo-Saxons would have done. The children learned to tease the fleece between their fingers, pulling it straight so that the fibres lay parallel. They let go of the wool so the spinning spindle twisted the fibres into a strong thread.

The children explored the weaving house. They found a big, upright loom standing against a wall. They worked out how the Anglo-Saxons wove their wool into widths of cloth on looms like this. The craft officer helped them with the weaving.

The children hung woollen threads from the wooden frame of the loom, just as Anglo-Saxon weavers would have done. They hung clay weights on the bottom of the threads to stretch them tight. They learned how to weave threads in and out from side to side to make the cloth. They pushed the threads down with bone beaters to give the cloth a close texture. They also found a small portable tablet loom similar to looms which the Anglo-Saxons used to make decorative edging for their cloth.

The large doughnut shape is an Anglo-Saxon clay loom weight from Stow. The smaller rings are spindle weights, called spindle-whorls. They are made of clay, bone or antler.

These braids in Anglo-Saxon patterns were woven on a modern tablet loom. The thread was dyed before it was woven. The Anglo-Saxons used many different dye plants such as woad which dyed cloth blue, madder which dyed it red, and weld which dyed it yellow.

25

Anglo-Saxon technology

The villagers had to grow or make everything they needed. They put most of their time and effort into feeding and sheltering themselves. But in winter, when they were not working so hard on the land, the villagers had time to carve antler and bone, and decorate pots.

Using a pole lathe

The springy pole pulls the string up, turning the wood in the other direction.

A length of string is twisted round the piece of wood.

A piece of wood shaped roughly with an axe is wedged between two uprights.

As the wood turns the chisel cuts out the shape of the bowl!

The treadle pulls the string down, turning the wood in one direction.

The Anglo-Saxons of Stow used pole lathes similar to this to make bowls and cups. The children were surprised to learn that this piece of technology was still in everyday use by woodworkers in 1940.

At first the villagers made things for their own immediate use. But as daily life became more organised they began to produce more items than they needed. They exchanged these items with travelling traders. The traders brought bronze, copper and silver from elsewhere in England, glass beads and containers from Germany, and even a cowrie shell from the Indian Ocean. The traders took away goods such as pottery and cloth which, we know from later writings, was highly prized all over Europe.

By the middle of the AD 500s some Anglo-Saxons became skilled in particular crafts. They stopped farming and made a living by taking their skills from village to village. We know about one of these travelling workers who made pots at Stow in AD 600. The pots have been found in many places in East Anglia. They can be recognised by special decorations the potter always used.

The children made pots in the Anglo-Saxon way by pinching out the shape in clay. The villagers made other pots by coiling lengths of rolled clay round and round.

These are pots and pot stamps from Stow. The potter pressed the carved ends of the antler pot stamps into the clay while it was still damp. The stamp gave a clue as to who made the pot. These Anglo-Saxon pots were fired in a bonfire covered with turf to keep oxygen out. This caused a chemical change which turned the clay black.

27

The end of the village

The children discovered that by AD 650 the village of Stow had been abandoned. The children wondered why the villagers left and where they went. They could not find any evidence that the village had ever been attacked. Stow had been a peaceful place.

By AD 600, Anglo-Saxon life had started to change. The Anglo-Saxon kings wanted to control where people lived so they could raise more taxes. They offered protection to people who moved to 'wics' or market towns. The children looked at a map. They found that Gippeswic (modern Ipswich) was not far from Stow. They wondered if some craftworkers from the village moved to the town, hoping to become rich by making goods to sell there.

At about the time the villagers left Stow, the Anglo-Saxon tribes in East Anglia joined together to form a kingdom. One of the kings is buried at Sutton Hoo, about 32 kilometres from Stow. The king's grave is a ship buried under a mound of earth. The fabulous jewelled objects and the great hoard of gold coins buried with him show how rich and powerful East Anglia must have been. This helmet is part of the treasure.

The helmet after it had been reconstructed. It is decorated with animals which symbolise bravery and strength. The helmet was probably never worn in battle but was a sign of the power of the king.

This boy is holding modern copies of an Anglo-Saxon spear and shield. He found them very heavy. Anglo-Saxon men could be called on to fight for their king. Some Anglo-Saxon men were buried with their spears and shields.

The children also learned that Christian missionaries landed in Kent in AD 597. The missionaries converted some Anglo-Saxon kings to Christianity. The children wondered if some villagers had become Christians too. Perhaps those villagers moved to nearby West Stow and joined the settlement around the new Christian church which had been built there.

We will never know what really happened, but each new find can help us to imagine life 1500 years ago a little more clearly.

How to find out more

Visits

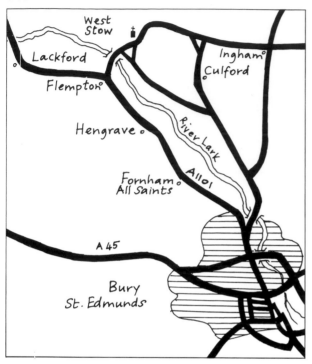

You can visit West Stow Anglo-Saxon Village and see practical archaeology at work. You can meet 'Anglo-Saxon' craftworkers and traders at special events held there. There are courses on traditional crafts such as using the pole lathe and weaving willow. Contact: The Visitor Centre, West Stow Country Park and Anglo-Saxon Village, Icklingham Road, West Stow, Bury St Edmunds, Suffolk IP18 6HG. Tel: 01284 728718.

Many of the finds from Stow are housed at Moyses Hall Museum, Bury St Edmunds. Your local museum may have a collection of Anglo-Saxon objects. To learn more about archaeology or working as a volunteer contact: The Young Archaeologists Club, The Council of British Archaeologists, Bowes Morrell House, 111 Walmgate, York YO1 9WA.

The Longship Trading Company, which features in this book, provides 'Living History' days where schools can experience Anglo-Saxon life by trying out replica clothes and tools of the period. Contact: The Longship Trading Company Ltd, 342 Albion Street, Wall Heath, Kingswinford, West Midlands DY6 0JR. Tel: 01384 292237.

Things to do

Here are some ideas for things to do which could help you to find out more about life in Anglo-Saxon times.

Make your own Anglo-Saxon beads

You will need: modelling clay in three different colours which can be baked in an oven; a nail; a thin leather thong or shoelace; a blunt knife.

Roll out three long sausage shapes of clay in different colours. Line them up beside each other, then plait or twist them together. Roll the plait into a flat sausage shape and cut it into bead-sized sections. Make a hole through the centre of each bead with the nail.

Bake the beads gently in the oven to harden them. Thread the beads onto the thong or shoe lace and wear them as a necklace.

Make your own Anglo-Saxon pot stamp

The Anglo-Saxons made their stamps out of wood, antler or bone. You could use a potato because it is easier to carve. Choose one of these Anglo-Saxon stamps for your design.

You will need: a small potato; poster paints; a plate; a piece of plain paper; a clay plant pot; a blunt knife.

Cut the potato in half. Mark your design on one of the cut surfaces with the tip of the knife. Scoop out the areas of the cut surface which are not part of the actual design.

Put a small amount of paint on the plate. Dip the cut surface of the potato into the paint. Press it against the paper a few times to see the effect. Try pressing the design on the clay pot to create a band going right round.

Invent an Anglo-Saxon riddle

The Anglo-Saxons were very fond of riddles. Here are two which have been handed down to us. Can you work out what each one refers to? The answers are on page 32. Try making up your own riddle.

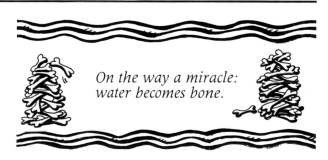

On the way a miracle: water becomes bone.

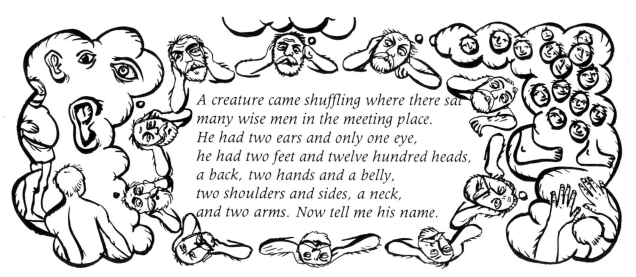

A creature came shuffling where there sat many wise men in the meeting place. He had two ears and only one eye, he had two feet and twelve hundred heads, a back, two hands and a belly, two shoulders and sides, a neck, and two arms. Now tell me his name.

Index

Reprinted 2002, 2003, 2007
First paperback edition 2000

First published 1994 in hardback
by A&C Black Publishers Ltd
38 Soho Square, London, W1D 3HB
www.acblack.com

ISBN:978-0-7136-5367-0

© 1994 A & C Black Publishers Ltd

A CIP catalogue record for this book is available from the British Library.

Books in the series:
Anglo-Saxon Village   Roman Palace
Home in the Blitz   Tudor Farmhouse
Roman Fort   Viking Street

Acknowledgements
The author and publishers would like to thank the staff at West Stow Country Park and Anglo-Saxon Village for their wholehearted support, especially Judith Roberts (Education Officer), Alan Baxter (Senior Ranger) and Will Wall (Crafts Officer); Dr Stanley West (excavator of the site, Suffolk County Archaeologist [retired]), who acted as quality controller; Chris Mycock (Museum Assistant at Moyses Hall Museum, Bury St Edmunds); David Crowther (Principal Museums Officer, St Edmundsbury Borough Council); the children in this book: Katheryn Brown, Sebastian Rodgers, Louise Mann, Amjad Khan from Claremont School, Nottingham, and Natalie Speake their teacher; Rebecca Almudevar, Freya Aitken-Turff, Jessica Gildersleeve; David Greenhalgh; members of the Longship Trading Company.

Photographs by Maggie Murray except for: p4 from the collection of Dr Stanley West; p5 (middle), 25 Borough of St Edmundsbury/ West Stow Anglo-Saxon Village Trust; pp9 (top), 11 Monica Stoppleman; p9 (bottom) Norwich Castle Museum, Norfolk Museums; pp19 (bottom), 20 (bottom) by permission of the British Library; pp28, 29 (left) C M Dixon.

Apart from any fair dealing for the purposes of research or private study, or criticism or review, as permitted under the Copyright Designs and Patents Act, 1988, this publication may be reproduced, stored or transmitted, in any form, or by any means, only with the prior permission in writing of the publishers, or, in the case of reprographic reproduction in accordance with the terms of licenses issued by the Copyright Licensing Agency. Inquiries concerning reproduction outside those terms should be sent to the publishers at the above named address.

Filmset by Rowland Phototypesetting Ltd, Bury St Edmunds, Suffolk.
This book is produced using paper made from wood grown in managed, sustainable forests. It is natural, renewable, and recyclable. The logging and manufacturing processes conform to the environmental regulations of the country of origin.
Printed and bound in China by Leo Paper Products.
Riddle answers: *Ice; a one-eyed seller of onions.*